The Wedding Book

Illuminated by Owen Jones

The Form of
Solemnization
of
Matrimony

Irst the Bawns of all that are to be married together, must be published in the Church three several Sundays during the time of Morning Service or of Evening Service (if there be no Morning Service,) immediately after the second Lesson; the Curate saying after the accustomed manner.

publish the banns of marriage between M. and N.

If any of you know cause or just impediment why these two persons should not be joined together in holy Matrimony, ye are to declare it This is the first (second or third) time of asking.

And if the persons that are to be married dwell in divers Parishes the Banns must be asked in both Parishes and the Curate of the one Parish shall not solemnize Matrimony betwixt them, without a Certificate of the Banns being thrice asked from the Curate of the other Parish.

At the day and time appointed for solemnization of Matrimony the persons to be married shall come into the body of the Church with their friends and neighbours and there standing together, the Man on the right hand, and the Woman on the left, the Priest shall say.

Dearly beloved, we are gathered together here in the sight of God and in the face of this congregation, to join together this Man and this Woman in Holy Matrimony which is an honorable estate, instituted of God in the time of men's innocency, signifying unto us the mystical union that is betwixt Christ and his Church which holy estate Christ adorned and beautified with his presence, and first

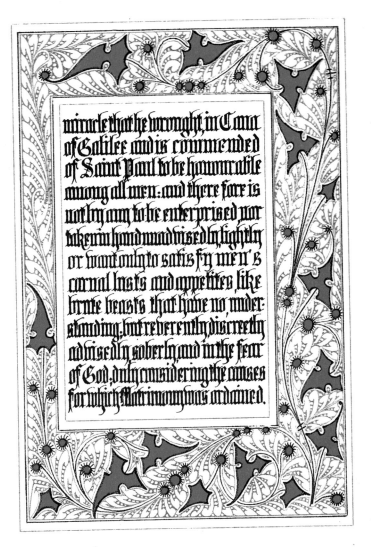

miracle that he wrought in Cana of Galilee and is commended of Saint Paul to be honourable among all men: and therefore is not by any to be enterprised nor taken in hand unadvisedly, lightly or wantonly to satisfy men's carnal lusts and appetites, like brute beasts that have no understanding, but reverently, discreetly, advisedly, soberly, and in the fear of God, duly considering the causes for which Matrimony was ordained.

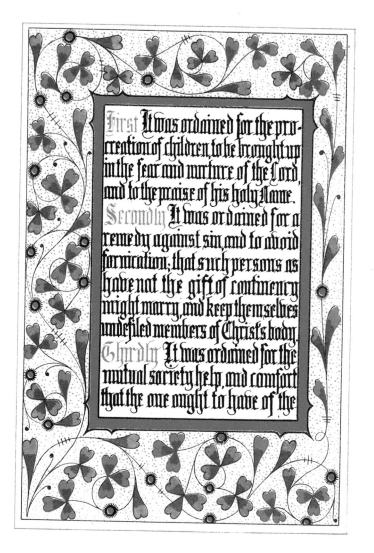

First It was ordained for the procreation of children, to be brought up in the fear and nurture of the Lord, and to the praise of his holy Name.

Secondly It was ordained for a remedy against sin, and to avoid fornication, that such persons as have not the gift of continency might marry, and keep themselves undefiled members of Christ's body.

Thirdly It was ordained for the mutual society, help, and comfort that the one ought to have of the

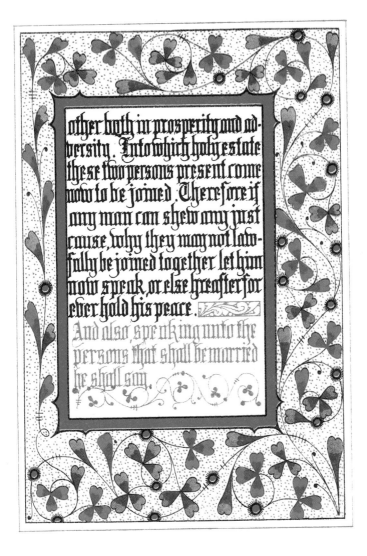

other both in prosperity and adversity. Into which holy estate these two persons present come now to be joined. Therefore if any man can shew any just cause, why they may not lawfully be joined together let him now speak, or else hereafter for ever hold his peace.

And also, speaking unto the persons that shall be married he shall say

I require and charge you both, as ye will answer at the dreadful day of judgement when the secrets of all hearts shall be disclosed, that if either of you know any impediment why ye may not be lawfully joined together in Matrimony, ye do now confess it. For be ye well assured that so many as are coupled together otherwise than God's Word doth

allow are not joined together by
God; neither is their Matrimony
lawful.

At which day of Marriage, if any
man do alledge and declare any
impediment, why then may not be
coupled together in Matrimony
by God's law, or the laws of this
Realm; and will be bound and
sufficient sureties with him to the
parties; or else put in a Caution
to the full value of such charges as
the persons to be married do there by

sustain) to prove his allegation
then the solemnization must be
deferred, until such time as the
truth be tried. ❧❧❧
If no impediment be alledged then
shall the Curate say unto the Man.

Mwilt thou have this
Woman to thy wed-
ded wife, to live toge-
ther after God's or-
dinance in the holy estate of
Matrimony? Wilt thou love her,
comfort her, honour and keep her

in sickness and in health, and forsaking all other keep thee only unto her, so long as ye both shall live?

The man shall answer,

I will.

Then shall the Priest say unto the Woman.

wilt thou have this Man to thy wedded husband, to live together after God's ordinance in the holy estate of Matrimony? Wilt thou obey him,

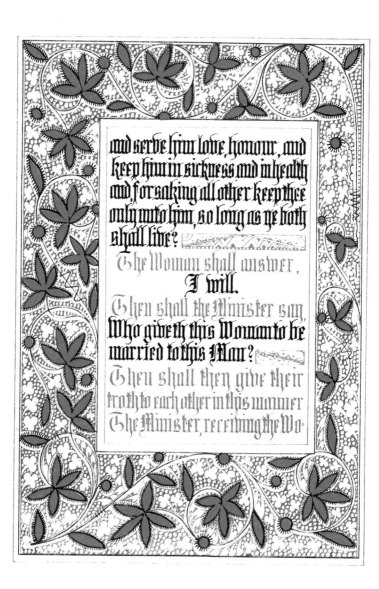

and serve him love, honour, and keep him in sickness and in health and forsaking all other keep thee only unto him, so long as ye both shall live?

The Woman shall answer,

I will.

Then shall the Minister say,

Who giveth this Woman to be married to this Man?

Then shall then give their troth to each other in this manner

The Minister, receiving the Wo-

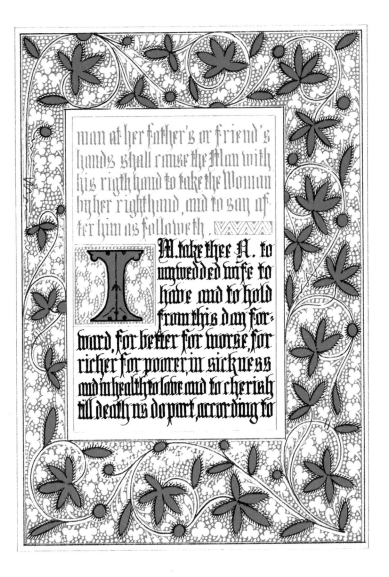

man at her father's or friend's hands shall cause the Man with his rigth hand to take the Woman by her righthand, and to say after him as followeth.

I M. take thee N. to my wedded wife to have and to hold from this day forward, for better for worse, for richer for poorer, in sickness and in health to love and to cherish till death us do part, according to

God's holy ordinance; and thereto I plight thee my troth.

Then shall they loose their hands and the Woman with her right hand taking the Man by his right hand shall likewise say after the Minister.

N. take thee M. to my wedded husband, to have and to hold from this day forward, for better for worse, for richer for poorer, in sickness and in health, to love cherish

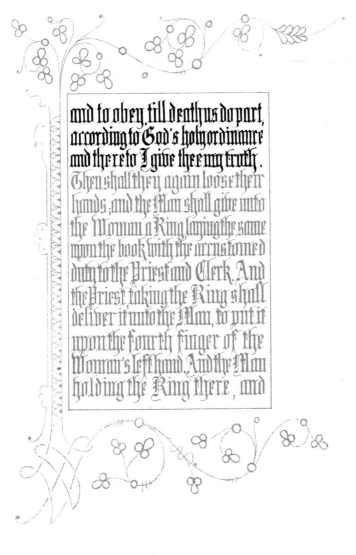

and to obey, till death us do part,
according to God's holy ordinance
and thereto I give thee my troth.
Then shall they again loose their
hands; and the Man shall give unto
the Woman a Ring, laying the same
upon the book with the accustomed
duty to the Priest and Clerk. And
the Priest taking the Ring shall
deliver it unto the Man, to put it
upon the fourth finger of the
Woman's left hand. And the Man
holding the Ring there, and

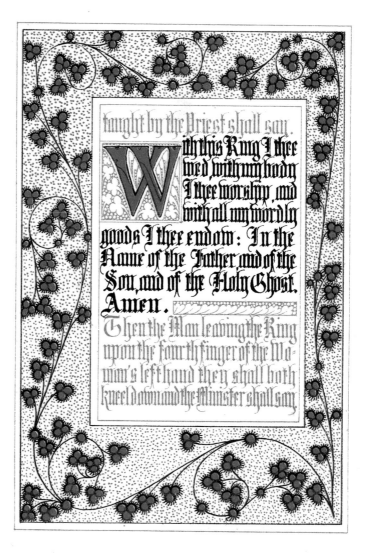

taught by the Priest shall say.

With this Ring I thee wed, with my body I thee worship, and with all my worldly goods I thee endow: In the Name of the Father, and of the Son, and of the Holy Ghost. Amen.

Then the Man leaving the Ring upon the fourth finger of the Woman's left hand they shall both kneel down and the Minister shall say

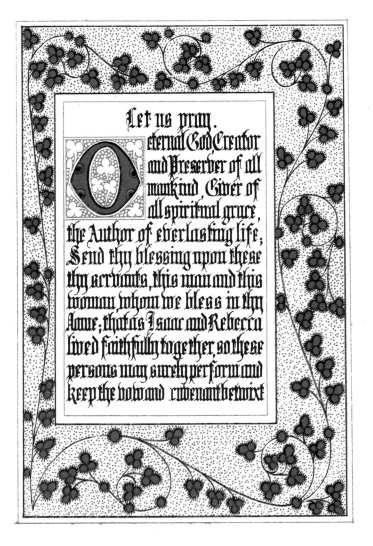

Let us pray.

O eternal God, Creator and Preserver of all mankind, Giver of all spiritual grace, the Author of everlasting life; Send thy blessing upon these thy servants, this man and this woman whom we bless in thy Name; that as Isaac and Rebecca lived faithfully together, so these persons may surely perform and keep the vow and covenant betwixt

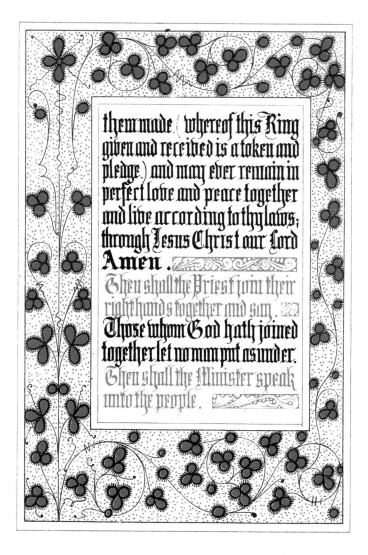

them made (whereof this Ring given and received is a token and pledge) and may ever remain in perfect love and peace together and live according to thy laws; through Jesus Christ our Lord Amen.

Then shall the Priest join their right hands together and say.

Those whom God hath joined together let no man put asunder.

Then shall the Minister speak unto the people.

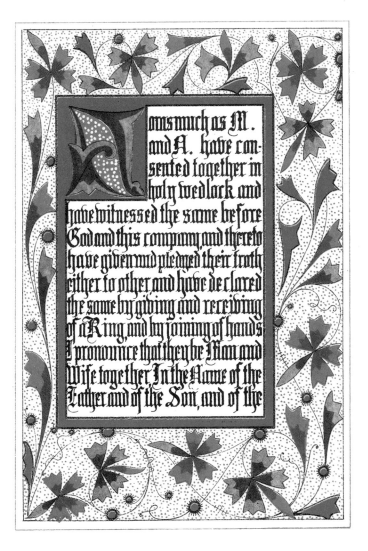

Forasmuch as M. and A. have consented together in holy wedlock and have witnessed the same before God and this company, and thereto have given and pledged their troth either to other and have declared the same by giving and receiving of a Ring, and by joining of hands I pronounce that they be Man and Wife together, In the Name of the Father and of the Son, and of the

Holy Ghost . Amen .

And the Minister shall add this Blessing.

God the Father God the Son, God the Holy Ghost bless, preserve and keep you, the Lord mercifully with his favour look upon you, and so fill you with all spiritual benediction and grace that ye may so live together in this life, that in the world to come ye may have life everlasting. Amen.

Then the Minister or Clerks going
to the Lord's Table, shall say or sing
this Psalm following.

Beati omnes. Psalm. CXXVIII.

Blessed are all they
that fear the Lord:
and walk in his ways

For thou shalt eat the
labour of thine hands: O well is thee,
and happy shalt thou be.

Thy wife shall be as the fruitful
vine: upon the walls of thine house;
Thy children like the olive-branches

round about thy table

Lo, thus shall the man be blessed
that feareth the Lord

The Lord from out of Sion shall
so bless thee: that thou shalt see
Jerusalem in prosperity all thy
life long

Yea that thou shalt see thy children's
children: and peace upon Israël

Glory be to the Father and to the Son
and to the Holy Ghost

As it was in the beginning is now
and ever shall be : world without

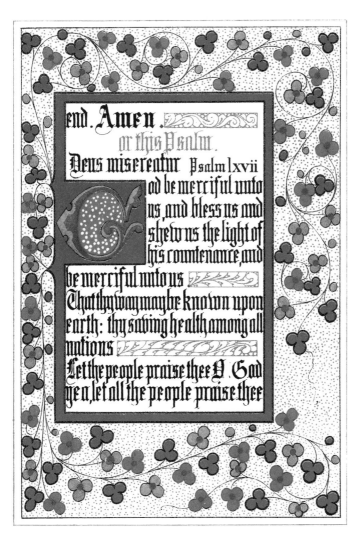

end. Amen.

or this Psalm.

Deus misereatur   Psalm lxvii

God be merciful unto us, and bless us and shew us the light of his countenance, and

be merciful unto us

That thy way may be known upon earth: thy saving health among all nations

Let the people praise thee O God ye a, let all the people praise thee

O let the nations rejoice and be glad
for thou shalt judge the folk right-
eously and govern the nations
upon earth.

Let the people praise thee, O God
yea, let all the people praise thee.

Then shall the earth bring forth her
increase and God even our own
God, shall give us his blessing.

God shall bless us: and all the ends
of the world shall fear him

Glory be to the Father and to the
Son, and to the Holy Ghost.

As it was in the beginning is now and ever shall be world without end. Amen.

The Psalm ended and the Man and the Woman kneeling before the Lord's Table, the Priest standing at the Table and turning his face towards them shall say.

Lord, have mercy upon us.

Answer.

Christ, have mercy upon us.

Minister.

Lord, have mercy upon us.

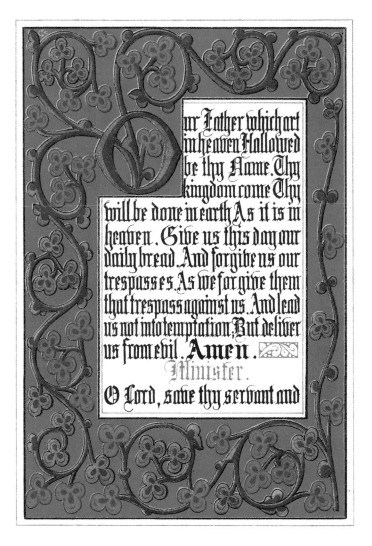

Our Father which art in heaven Hallowed be thy Name. Thy kingdom come Thy will be done in earth As it is in heaven. Give us this day our daily bread. And forgive us our trespasses As we forgive them that trespass against us. And lead us not into temptation; But deliver us from evil. **Amen**.

Minister.

O Lord, save thy servant and

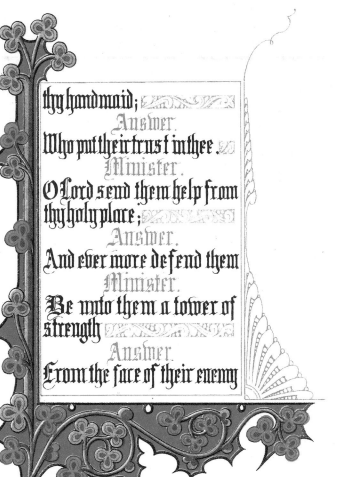

thy handmaid;

Answer.

Who put their trust in thee.

Minister.

O Lord send them help from thy holy place;

Answer.

And ever more defend them

Minister.

Be unto them a tower of strength

Answer.

From the face of their enemy

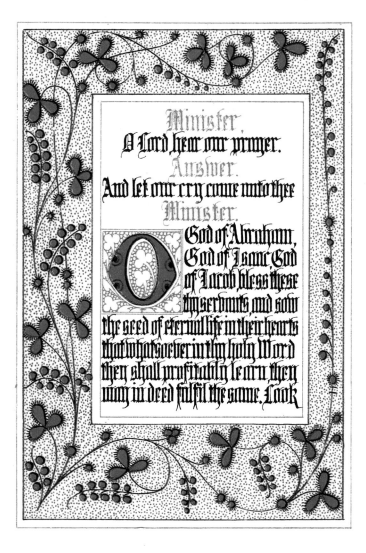

Minister.

O Lord hear our prayer.

Answer.

And let our cry come unto thee

Minister.

O God of Abraham, God of Isaac, God of Jacob bless these thy servants, and sow the seed of eternal life in their hearts, that whatsoever in thy holy Word they shall profitably learn, they may in deed fulfil the same. Look

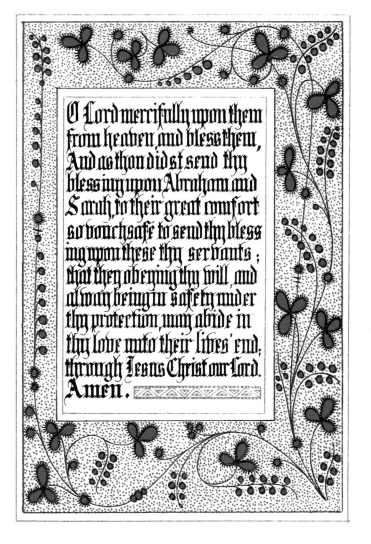

O Lord mercifully upon them from heaven, and bless them, And as thou didst send thy blessing upon Abraham and Sarah, to their great comfort so vouchsafe to send thy blessing upon these thy servants; that they obeying thy will, and alway being in safety under thy protection, may abide in thy love unto their lives' end, through Jesus Christ our Lord. Amen.

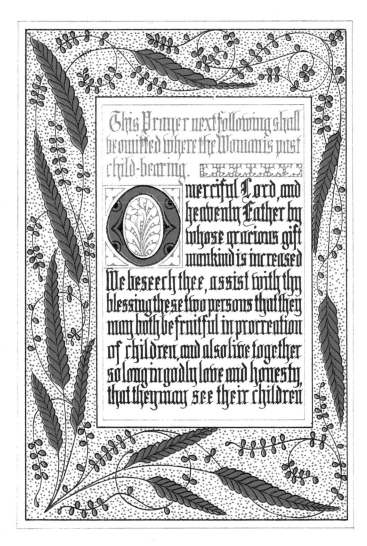

This Prayer next following shall be omitted where the Woman is past child-bearing.

O merciful Lord, and heavenly Father by whose gracious gift mankind is increased We beseech thee, assist with thy blessing these two persons that they may both be fruitful in procreation of children, and also live together so long in godly love and honesty, that they may see their children

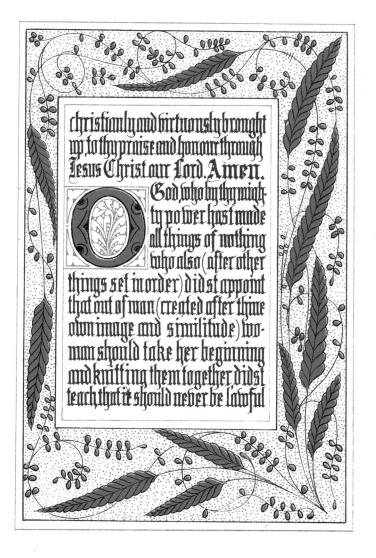

christianly and virtuously brought
up to thy praise and honour through
Jesus Christ our Lord. Amen.

O God, who by thy migh-
ty power hast made
all things of nothing,
who also (after other
things set in order) didst appoint
that out of man (created after thine
own image and similitude) woman should take her beginning,
and knitting them together didst
teach that it should never be lawful

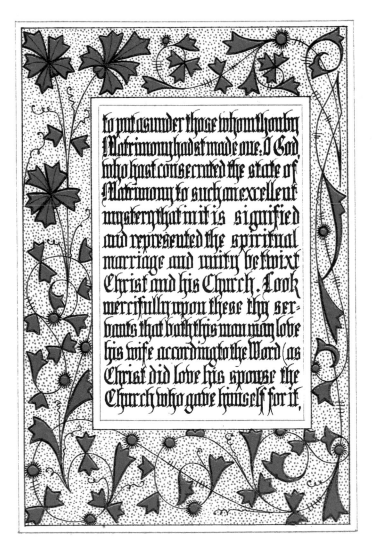

to put asunder those whom thou by Matrimony hadst made one. O God, who hast consecrated the state of Matrimony to such an excellent mystery, that in it is signified and represented the spiritual marriage and unity betwixt Christ and his Church. Look mercifully upon these thy servants that both this man may love his wife according to the Word (as Christ did love his spouse the Church who gave himself for it,

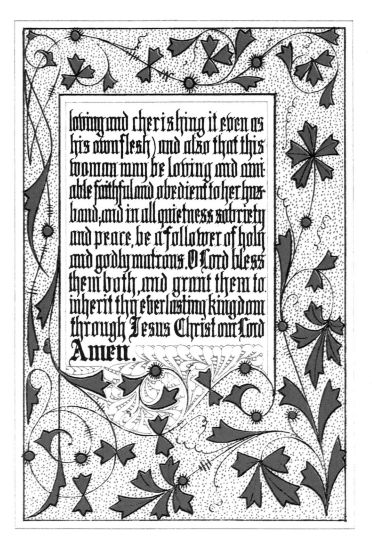

loving and cherishing it even as his own flesh,) and also that this woman may be loving and amiable faithful and obedient to her husband, and in all quietness sobriety and peace, be a follower of holy and godly matrons. O Lord bless them both, and grant them to inherit thy everlasting kingdom through Jesus Christ our Lord Amen.

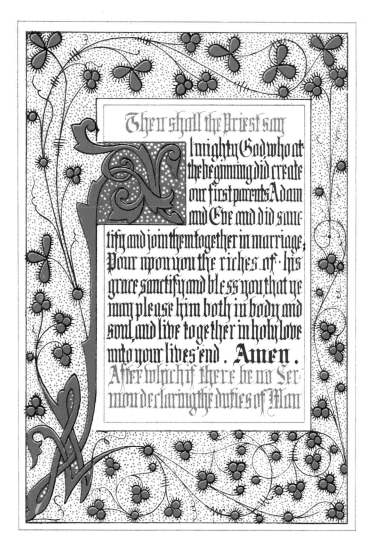

Then shall the Priest say

Almighty God who at the beginning did create our first parents Adam and Eve and did sanctify and join them together in marriage, Pour upon you the riches of his grace sanctify and bless you that ye may please him both in body and soul, and live together in holy love unto your lives' end. **Amen**.

After which if there be no Sermon declaring the duties of Man and Wife the Minister shall read as followeth.

All ye that are married, or that intend to take the holy estate of Matrimony upon you hear what the holy Scripture doth say as touching the duty of husbands towards their wives and wives towards their husbands Saint Paul in his Epistle to the Ephesians the fifth Chapter doth give this commandment to all

married men; Husbands, love your wives, even as Christ also loved the Church, and gave himself for it: that he might sanctify and cleanse it with the washing of water by the Word, that he might present it to himself a glorious Church, not having spot or wrinkle or any such thing, but that it should be holy and without blemish. So ought men to love their wives as their own bodies. He that loveth his wife loveth

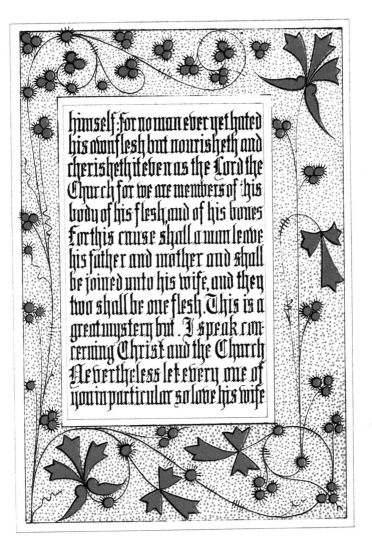

himself: for no man ever yet hated his own flesh but nourisheth and cherisheth it even as the Lord the Church for we are members of his body of his flesh, and of his bones For this cause shall a man leave his father and mother and shall be joined unto his wife, and they two shall be one flesh. This is a great mystery but . I speak concerning Christ and the Church Nevertheless let every one of you in particular so love his wife

even as himself.

Likewise the same Saint Paul writing to the Colossians speaketh thus to all men that are married; Husbands, love your wives, and be not bitter against them.

Hear also what Saint Peter, the Apostle of Christ who was himself a married man, saith unto them that are married; Ye husbands, dwell with your wives according to knowledge, giving honour unto the wife, as unto the weaker ves-

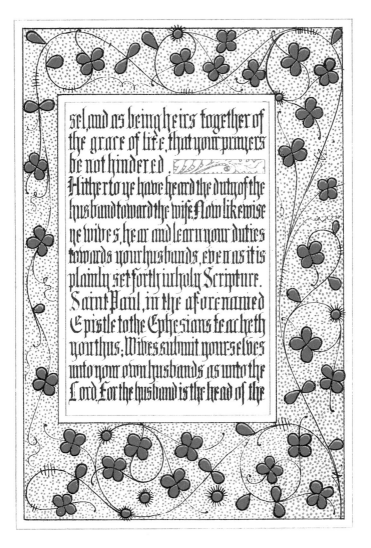

sel, and as being heirs together of
the grace of life, that your prayers
be not hindered.

Hitherto ye have heard the duty of the
husband toward the wife. Now likewise
ye wives, hear and learn your duties
towards your husbands, even as it is
plainly set forth in holy Scripture.
Saint Paul, in the aforenamed
Epistle to the Ephesians teacheth
you thus; Wives submit yourselves
unto your own husbands as unto the
Lord. For the husband is the head of the

wife even as Christ is the head of the Church: and he is the Saviour of the body. Therefore as the Church is subject unto Christ, so let the wives be to their own husbands in every thing. And again he saith Let the wife see that she reverence her husband.

And in his Epistle to the Colossians Saint Paul giveth you this short lesson, Wives submit your selves unto your own husbands, as it is fit in the Lord.

Saint Peter also doth instruct you very well thus saying; Ye wives be in subjection to your own husbands that if any obey not the Word they also may without the Word be won by the conversation of the wives; while they behold your chaste conversation coupled with fear. Whose adorning, let it not be that outward adorning of plaiting the hair, and of wearing of gold or of putting on of apparel but let it be the hidden man of the heart, in that which is not corruptible;

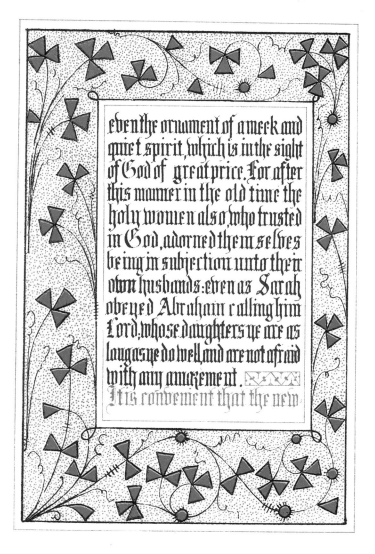

even the ornament of a meek and
quiet spirit, which is in the sight
of God of great price. For after
this manner in the old time the
holy women also, who trusted
in God, adorned themselves
being in subjection unto their
own husbands: even as Sarah
obeyed Abraham calling him
Lord, whose daughters ye are as
long as ye do well, and are not afraid
with any amazement.
It is convenient that the new

married persons should re-
ceive the holy Communion
at the time of their Marriage
or at the first opportunity after
their Marriage.

First published as *Holy Matrimony* by Longman & Co, 1849.

This Edition published 1990 by Wordsworth Editions Ltd,
8b East Street, Ware, Hertfordshire.

Copyright © Wordsworth Editions Ltd 1990.

ISBN 1-85326-945-X

Printed and bound in Spain by Gráficas Estella, S.A.